The Will to Change

ADRIENNE RICH

The Will to Change

Poems 1968-1970

W · W · NORTON & COMPANY · INC ·
NEW YORK

Some of these poems have appeared in the following periodicals: "November 1968," "Study of History," and "I Dream I'm the Death of Orpheus" in *Colloquy;* "Planetarium" in *Aphra* and *Inside Outer Space;* "The Burning of Paper Instead of Children" in *Caterpillar;* "Pierrot Le Fou" in *Field;* "Letters: March 1969" in *Harper's Magazine;* "Pieces" in *Salmagundi;* "Our Whole Life" in *The New Republic;* "The Stelae" in *New York Quarterly;* "The Photograph of the Unmade Bed" in *First Issue, No. 4.*

FIRST EDITION

Library of Congress Catalog Card No. 78-146842

SBN   393   04346   0   (Cloth Edition)

SBN   393   04361   4   (Paper Edition)

PRINTED IN THE UNITED STATES OF AMERICA

1 2 3 4 5 6 7 8 9 0

For David, Pablo and Jacob

What does not change/is the will to change
—Charles Olson, "The Kingfishers"

Contents

The Will to Change

November 1968

Stripped
you're beginning to float free
up through the smoke of brushfires
and incinerators
the unleafed branches won't hold you
nor the radar aerials

You're what the autumn knew would happen
after the last collapse
of primary color
once the last absolutes were torn to pieces
you could begin

How you broke open, what sheathed you
until this moment
I know nothing about it
my ignorance of you amazes me
now that I watch you
starting to give yourself away
to the wind

1968

Study of History

Out there.   The mind of the river
as it might be you.

Lights   blotted by unseen hulls
repetitive shapes passing
dull foam crusting the margin
barges sunk below the water-line with silence.
The scow, drudging on.

Lying in the dark, to think of you
and your harsh traffic
gulls pecking your rubbish   natural historians
mourning your lost purity
pleasure cruisers
witlessly careening you

but this
after all
is the narrows and after
all we have never entirely
known what was done to you upstream
what powers trepanned
which of your channels diverted
what rockface leaned to stare
in your upturned
defenseless
face.

1968

Planetarium

(*Thinking of Caroline
Herschel, 1750–1848,
astronomer, sister of
William;   and others*

A woman in the shape of a monster
a monster in the shape of a woman
the skies are full of them

a woman   'in the snow
among the Clocks and instruments
or measuring the ground with poles'

in her 98 years to discover
8 comets

she whom the moon ruled
like us
levitating into the night sky
riding the polished lenses

Galaxies of women, there
doing penance for impetuousness
ribs chilled
in those spaces   of the mind

An eye,
          'virile, precise and, absolutely certain'
          from the mad webs of Uranisborg

                              encountering the NOVA

every impulse of light exploding
from the core
as life flies out of us

Tycho whispering at last
'Let me not seem to have lived in vain'

What we see, we see
and seeing is changing

the light that shrivels a mountain
and leaves a man alive

Heartbeat of the pulsar
heart sweating through my body

The radio impulse
pouring in from Taurus

     I am bombarded yet   I stand

I have been standing all my life in the
direct path of a battery of signals
the most accurately transmitted most
untranslateable language in the universe
I am a galactic cloud so deep   so invo-
luted that a light wave could take 15
years to travel through me   And has
taken   I am an instrument in the shape
of a woman trying to translate pulsations
into images   for the relief of the body
and the reconstruction of the mind.

1968

The Burning of Paper
Instead of Children

I was in danger of
verbalizing my moral
impulses out of
existence.
—Fr. Daniel Berrigan,
on trial in Baltimore.

1.   My neighbor, a scientist and art-collector, telephones me in a
state of violent emotion. He tells me that my son and his, aged
eleven and twelve, have on the last day of school burned a mathe-
matics text-book in the backyard. He has forbidden my son to come
to his house for a week, and has forbidden his own son to leave the
house during that time. "The burning of a book," he says, "arouses
terrible sensations in me, memories of Hitler; there are few things
that upset me so much as the idea of burning a book."

Back there: the library, walled
with green Britannicas
Looking again
in Dürer's *Complete Works*
for MELANCOLIA, the baffled woman

the crocodiles in Herodotus
the Book of the Dead
the *Trial of Jeanne d'Arc,* so blue
I think, It is her color

and they take the book away
because I dream of her too often

love and fear in a house
knowledge of the oppressor

I know it hurts to burn

2.   To imagine a time of silence
or few words
a time of chemistry and music

the hollows above your buttocks
traced by my hand
or, *hair is like flesh,* you said

an age of long silence

relief

from this tongue   the slab of limestone
or reinforced concrete
fanatics and traders
dumped on this coast   wildgreen   clayred
that breathed once
in signals of smoke
sweep of the wind

knowledge of the oppressor
this is the oppressor's language

yet I need it to talk to you

3.   "People suffer highly in poverty and it takes dignity and intelli-
gence to overcome this suffering. Some of the suffering are: a child
did not had dinner last night: a child steal because he did not have
money to buy it: to hear a mother say she do not have money to buy
food for her children and to see a child without cloth it will make
tears in your eyes."

(the fracture of order
the repair of speech
to overcome this suffering)

4.   We lie under the sheet
after making love, speaking
of loneliness
relieved in a book
relived in a book
so on that page
the clot and fissure
of it appears
words of a man
in pain
a naked word
entering the clot
a hand grasping
through bars:

deliverance

What happens between us
has happened for centuries
we know it from literature

still it happens

sexual jealousy
outflung hand
beating bed

dryness of mouth
after panting

there are books that describe all this
and they are useless

You walk into the woods behind a house
there in that country
you find a temple
built eighteen hundred years ago
you enter without knowing
what it is you enter

so it is with us

no one knows what may happen
though the books tell everything

burn the texts   said Artaud

5.   I am composing on the typewriter late at night, thinking of
today. How well we all spoke. A language is a map of our failures.
Frederick Douglass wrote an English purer than Milton's. People
suffer highly in poverty. There are methods but we do not use them.
Joan, who could not read, spoke some peasant form of French.
Some of the suffering are: it is hard to tell the truth; this is America;
I cannot touch you now. In America we have only the present tense.
I am in danger. You are in danger. The burning of a book arouses
no sensation in me. I know it hurts to burn. There are flames of
napalm in Catonsville, Maryland. I know it hurts to burn. The
typewriter is overheated, my mouth is burning, I cannot touch you
and this is the oppressor's language.

1968

I Dream
I'm the Death of Orpheus

I am walking rapidly through striations of light and dark thrown
    under an arcade.

I am a woman in the prime of life, with certain powers
and those powers severely limited
by authorities whose faces I rarely see.
I am a woman in the prime of life
driving her dead poet in a black Rolls-Royce
through a landscape of twilight and thorns.
A woman with a certain mission
which if obeyed to the letter will leave her intact.
A woman with the nerves of a panther
a woman with contacts among Hell's Angels
a woman feeling the fullness of her powers
at the precise moment when she must not use them
a woman sworn to lucidity
who sees through the mayhem, the smoky fires
of these underground streets
her dead poet learning to walk backward against the wind
on the wrong side of the mirror

1968

The Blue Ghazals

9/21/68

Violently asleep in the old house.
A clock stays awake all night ticking.

Turning, turning their bruised leaves
the trees stay awake all night in the wood.

Talk to me with your body through my dreams.
Tell me what we are going through.

The walls of the room are muttering,
old trees, old Utopians, arguing with the wind.

To float like a dead man in a sea of dreams
and half those dreams being dreamed by someone else.

Fifteen years of sleepwalking with you,
wading against the tide, and with the tide.

9/23/68

One day of equinoctial light after another,
moving ourselves through gauzes and fissures of that light.

Early and late I come and set myself against you,
your phallic fist knocking blindly at my door.

The dew is beaded like mercury on the coarsened grass,
the web of the spider is heavy as if with sweat.

Everything is yielding toward a foregone conclusion,
only we are rash enough to go on changing our lives.

An Ashanti woman tilts the flattened basin on her head
to let the water slide downward: I am that woman and that
        water.

9/28/68: i

A man, a woman, a city.
The city as object of love.

Anger and filth in the basement.
The furnace stoked and blazing.

A sexual heat on the pavements.
Trees erected like statues.

Eyes at the ends of avenues.
Yellow for hesitation.

I'm tired of walking your streets
he says, unable to leave her.

Air of dust and rising sparks,
the city burning her letters.

9/28/68: ii   (*For Wallace Stevens.*

Ideas of order . . . Sinner of the Florida keys,
you were our poet of revolution all along.

A man isn't what he seems but what he desires:
gaieties of anarchy drumming at the base of the skull.

Would this have left you cold, our scene, its wild parades,
the costumes, banners, incense, flowers, the immense marches?

Disorder is natural, these leaves absently blowing
in the drinking-fountain, filling the statue's crevice.

The use of force in public architecture:
nothing, not even the honeycomb, manifests such control.

9/29/68   *(For LeRoi Jones.*

Late at night I went walking through your difficult wood,
half-sleepy, half-alert in that thicket of bitter roots.

Who doesn't speak to me, who speaks to me more and more,
but from a face turned off, turned away, a light shut out.

Most of the old lecturers are inaudible or dead.
Prince of the night there are explosions in the hall.

The blackboard scribbled over with dead languages
is falling and killing our children.

Terribly far away I saw your mouth in the wild light:
it seemed to me you were shouting instructions to us all.

12/13/68

They say, if you can tell, clasped tight under the blanket,
the edge of dark from the edge of dawn, your love is a lie.

If I thought of my words as changing minds,
hadn't my mind also to suffer changes?

They measure fever, swab the blisters of the throat,
but the cells of thought go rioting on ignored.

It's the inner ghost that suffers, little spirit
looking out wildly from the clouded pupils.

When will we lie clearheaded in our flesh again
with the cold edge of the night driving us close together?

12/20/68: i

There are days when I seem to have nothing
but these frayed packets, done up with rotting thread.

The shortest day of the year, let it be ours.
Let me give you something: a token for the subway.

(Refuse even
the most beloved old solutions.

That dead man wrote, grief ought to reach the lips.
You must believe I know before you can tell me.

A black run through the tunnelled winter, he and she,
together, touching, yet not side by side.

12/20/68: ii

Frost, burning. The city's ill.
We gather like viruses.

The doctors are all on their yachts
watching the beautiful skin-divers.

The peasant mind of the Christian
transfixed on food at the year's turning.

Thinking of marzipan
forget that revolutionary child.

Thought grown senile with sweetness.
You too may visit the Virgins.

In the clear air, hijacked planes
touch down at the forbidden island.

5/4/69

Pain made her conservative.
Where the matches touched her flesh, she wears a scar.

The police arrive at dawn
like death and childbirth.

City of accidents, your true map
is the tangling of all our lifelines.

The moment when a feeling enters the body
is political. This touch is political.

Sometimes I dream we are floating on water
hand-in-hand; and sinking without terror.

Pierrot Le Fou

1.
Suppose you stood facing
a wall
     of photographs
from your unlived life

as you stand looking at these
stills from the unseen film?

Yourself against a wall
curiously stuccoed

Yourself in the doorway
of a kind of watchman's hut

Yourself at a window
signalling to people
you haven't met yet

Yourself in unfamiliar clothes
with the same eyes

2.
On a screen as wide as this, I grope for the titles.
I speak the French language like a schoolgirl of the 'forties.
Those roads remind me of Beauce and the motorcycle.
We rode from Paris to Chartres in the March wind.
He said we should go to Spain but the wind defeated me.
France of the superhighways, I never knew you.
How much the body took in those days, and could take!
A naked lightbulb still simmers in my eyeballs.
In every hotel, I lived on the top floor.

3.
Suppose we had time
and no money

living by our wits
                  telling stories

which stories would you tell?

I would tell the story
of Pierrot Le Fou
who trusted
                  not a woman
                            but love itself

till his head blew off
not quite intentionally

I would tell all the stories I knew
in which people went wrong
but the nervous system

was right all along

4.
The island blistered our feet.
At first we mispronounced each others' names.
All the leaves of the tree were scribbled with words.
There was a language there but no-one to speak it.
Sometimes each of us was alone.
At noon on the beach our shadows left us.
The net we twisted from memory kept on breaking.
The damaged canoe lay on the beach like a dead animal.
You started keeping a journal on a coconut shell.

5.
When I close my eyes
other films
                  have been there all along

a market shot:
bins of turnips, feet
of dead chickens

close-up: a black old woman
buying voodoo medicines

a figure of terrible faith
and I know her needs

Another film:
                an empty room stacked with old films
I am kneeling on the floor
it is getting dark
                they want to close the building
and I still haven't found you

Scanning reel after reel
tundras in negative,
the Bowery
            all those scenes

but the light is failing
                    and you are missing
from the footage of the march
the railway disaster
the snowbound village

even the shots of the island
miss you
        yet you were there

6.
To record
in order to see

                        if you know how the story ends
                        why tell it

To record
in order to forget

                        the surface is always lucid
                        my shadows are under the skin

27

To record
in order to control

> the eye of the camera
> doesn't weep tears of blood

To record
for that is what one does

> climbing your stairs, over and over
> I memorized the bare walls

> This is my way of coming back

1969

Letters: March 1969

Foreknown. The victor
sees the disaster through and through.
His soles grind rocksalt
from roads of the resistance.
He shoulders through rows
of armored faces
he might have loved and lived among.
The victory carried like a corpse
from town to town
begins to crawl in the casket.
The summer swindled on
from town to town, our train
stopping and broiling on the rails
long enough to let on who we were.
The disaster sat up with us all night
drinking bottled water, eating fruit,
talking of the conditions that prevailed.
Outside along the railroad cut
they were singing for our death.

Hopes sparkle like water in the clean carafe.
How little it takes
to restore composure.
White napkins, a tray
of napoleons and cherry tarts
compliments of the airline
which has flown us out of danger.
They are torturing the journalist we drank with
last night in the lounge
but we can't be sure of that

here overlooking the runway
three hours and twenty minutes into another life.
If this is done for us
(and this is done for us)
if we are well men wearing bandages
for disguise
if we can choose our scene
stay out of earshot
break the roll and pour
from the clean carafe
if we can desert like soldiers
abjure like thieves
we may well purchase new virtues at the gate
of the other world.

3.

"I am up at sunrise
collecting data.
The reservoir burns green.
Darling, the knives they have on this block alone
would amaze you.
When they ask my profession I say
I'm a student of weapons systems.
The notes I'm putting together are purely
of sentimental value
my briefcase is I swear useless
to foreign powers, to the police
I am not given I say
to revealing my sources
to handing round copies
of my dossier for perusal.
The vulnerable go unarmed.
I myself walk the floor
a ruinously expensive Swiss hunter's knife
exposed in my brain

eight blades, each one for a distinct purpose,
laid open as on the desk
of an importer or a fence."

4.

Six months back
send carbons you said
but this winter's dashed off in pencil
torn off the pad too fast
for those skills. In the dawn taxi
in the kitchen
burning the succotash
the more I love my life the more
I love you. In a time
of fear. In a city
of fears. In a life
without vacations the paisley fades
winter and summer in the sun
but the best time is now.

My sick friend writes: *what's love?*
This life is nothing, Adrienne!

Her hands bled onto the sill.
She had that trick of reaching outward,
the pane was smashed but only
the calvinist northwind
spat in from the sea.
She's a shot hero. A dying poet.
Even now, if we went for her—
but they've gone with rags and putty to fix the pane.
She stays in with her mirrors and anger.

I tear up answers
I once gave, postcards
from riot and famine go up on the walls

valentines stuck in the mirror
flame and curl, loyalties dwindle
the bleak light dries our tears
without relief. I keep coming back to you

in my head, but you couldn't know that, and
I have no carbons. Prince of pity,
what eats out of your hand?
the rodent pain, electric
with exhaustion, mazed and shaken?
I'd have sucked the wound in your hand to sleep
but my lips were trembling.
Tell me how to bear myself,
how it's done, the light kiss falling
accurately
on the cracked palm.

1969

Pieces

1. *Breakpoint*

The music of words
received as fact

The steps that wouldn't hold us both
splintering in air

The self witheld in an urn
like ashes

To have loved you better than you loved yourself
—whoever you were, to have loved you—

And still to love but simply
as one of those faces on the street

2. *Relevance*

That erudition
how to confront it

The critics wrote answers
the questions were ours

A breast, a shoulder
chilled at waking

The cup of yoghurt
eaten at noon
and no explanations

The books we borrowed
trying to read each other's minds

Paperbacks piling
on both sides of the fireplace
and piled beside the bed

What difference could it make
that those books came
out of unintelligible pain

as daylight out of the hours

when that light burned
atop the insurance tower
all night like the moon

3. *Memory*

Plugged-in to her body
he came the whole way
but it makes no difference

If not this then what
would fuse a connection

(All that burning intelligence about love
what can it matter

Falling in love on words
and ending in silence
with its double-meanings

Always falling and ending
because this world gives no room
to be what we dreamt of being

Are we, as he said
of the generation that forgets
the lightning-flash, the air-raid

and each other

4. *Time and Place*

Liquid mist burning off
along the highway

Slap of water
Light on shack boards

Hauling of garbage
early in the wet street

Always the same, wherever waking,
the old positions
assumed by the mind

and the new day forms
like a china cup

hard, cream-colored, unbreakable
even in our travels

5. *Revelation*

This morning: read Simone Weil
on the loss of grace

drank a glass of water

remembered the dream that woke me:

some one, some more than one
battering into my room
intent to kill me

I crying your name
its two syllables
ringing through sleep

knowing it vain
knowing
you slept unhearing

crying your name
like a spell

like signs executed

by the superstitious

who are the faithful of this world

1969

Our Whole Life

Our whole life a translation
the permissible fibs

and now a knot of lies
eating at itself to get undone

Words bitten thru words

meanings burnt-off like paint
under the blowtorch

All those dead letters
rendered into the oppressor's language

Trying to tell the doctor where it hurts
like the Algerian
who has walked from his village, burning

his whole body a cloud of pain
and there are no words for this

except himself

1969

Your Letter

                blinds me
like the light of that surf
you thrust your body in
for punishment

or the river of fiery fenders
and windshields
you pour yourself into
driving north to S.F.
on that coast of chrome and oil

I watch for any signal
the tremor of courage
in the seismograph

a flash
where I thought the glare
was steady, smogged & tame

1969

Stand up in my nightgown at the window
almost naked behind black glass

Off from the line of trees the road
beaten, bare, we walked

in the light of the bare, beaten moon.
Almost, you spoke to me. The road

swings past swampground
the soft spots of the earth

you might sink through into location
where their cameras are set up

the underground film-makers waiting to make their film
waiting for you

their cameras pivot toward your head and the film burns
but you're not talking

If I am there you have forgotten my name
you think perhaps 'a woman'

and you drift on, drifter, through the frames
of the movie they are making of this time.

A whole soundtrack of your silence
a whole film

of dark nights and darker rooms
and blank sheets of paper, bare . . .

1969

The Stelae

(*For Arnold Rich.*

Last night I met you in my sister's house
risen from the dead
showing me your collection

You are almost at the point of giving things away

It's the stelae on the walls I want
that I never saw before

You offer other objects
I have seen time and time again

I think you think you are giving me
something precious

The stelae are so unlike you
swart, indifferent, incised with signs
you have never deciphered

I never knew you had them
I wonder if you are giving them away

1969

Snow

when it comes down turning
itself in clusters before the flat
light of the shortest day

you see how all turns away
from us how we turn
into our shadows you can see
how we are tested

the individual crystal on the
black skirt of the maxi-coat
under the lens

was it a whole day or just a lifetime
spent studying crystals

on the fire escape while the 'Sixties
were running out
could you see

how the black ladder spun away from us
into whiteness
how over and over
a star became a tear

if no two are alike
then what are we doing
with these diagrams of loss

1969

The Will to Change

1.   (*For L. D.,
                                      dead 11/69.*

That Chinese restaurant was a joke
with its repeating fountains

& chopsticks in tissue paper
The vodka was too sweet

the beancurd too hot
You came with your Egyptian hieroglyph

your angel's smile
Almost the next day

as surely as if shot
you were thin air

At the risk of appearing ridiculous—
we take back this halfworld for you

and all whose murders accrue
past your death

2.   (*For Sandra Levinson.*
Knocked down in the canefield
by a clumsily swung machete

she is helped to her feet
by Fidel

and snapped by photographers
the blonde Yanqui in jeans

We're living through a time
that needs to be lived through us

42

(and in the morning papers
Bobby Seale, chalked

by the courtroom artist
defaced by the gag)

3.   *(For D. J. L.*
Beardless again, phoning
from a storefront in Yorkville

. . . we need a typewriter, a crib
& Michael's number . . .

I swim to you thru dead
latitudes of fever   ,

. . . accepting the discipline . . .
You mean your old freedom

to disappear—you miss that?
. . . but I can dig having lost it . . .

David, I could dig losing everything.
Knowing what you mean, to make that leap

bite into the fear, over & over
& survive. Hoarding my 'liberty'

like a compulsive—more
than I can use up in a lifetime—

two dozen oranges in the refrigerator
for one American weekend

4.   *(For A. H. C.*
At the wings of the mirror, peacock plumes
from the Feast of San Gennaro

gaze thru the dark
All night the A-train forages

43

under our bedroom
All night I dream of a man

black, gagged, shackled, coffined
in a courtroom where I am

passive, white & silent
though my mouth is free

All night I see his eyes
iridescent under torture

and hear the shuddering of the earth
as the trains tear us apart

5.
The cabdriver from the Bronx
screaming: 'This city's GOTTA die!'

dynamiting it hourly from his soul
as surely as any terrorist

Burning the bodies of the scum on welfare
ejaculating into the flames

(*and,* said Freud,
who welcomed it when it was done?)

the professors of the fact
that someone has suffered

seeking truth in a mist of librium
the artists talking of freedom

in their chains

1969–1970

The Photograph of the Unmade Bed

Cruelty is rarely conscious
One slip of the tongue

one exposure
among so many

a thrust in the dark
to see if there's pain there

I never asked you to explain
that act of violence

what dazed me was our ignorance
of our will to hurt each other

. . . . . .

In a flash I understand
how poems are unlike photographs

(the one saying   This could be
the other   This was

The image
isn't responsible

for our uses of it
It is intentionless

A long strand of dark hair
in the washbasin

is innocent and yet
such things have done harm

. . . . . .

45

These snapshots taken by ghetto children
given for Christmas

Objects blurring into perceptions
No 'art,' only the faults

of the film, the faults of the time
Did mere indifference blister

these panes, eat these walls,
shrivel and scrub these trees—

mere indifference? I tell you
cruelty is rarely conscious

the done and the undone blur
into one photograph of failure

        . . . . . .

This crust of bread we try to share
this name traced on a window

this word I paste together
like a child fumbling

with paste and scissors
this writing in the sky with smoke

this silence

this lettering chalked on the ruins
this alphabet of the dumb

this feather held to lips
that still breathe and are warm

1969

Images for Godard

1. Language as city:: Wittgenstein
    Driving to the limits
    of the city of words

    the superhighway streams
    like a comic strip

    to newer suburbs
    casements of shockproof glass

    where no one yet looks out
    or toward the coast where even now

    the squatters in their shacks
    await eviction

    When all conversation
    becomes an interview
    under duress

    when we come to the limits
    of the city

    my face must have a meaning

2. To know the extremes of light
    I sit in this darkness

    To see the present flashing
    in a rearview mirror

    blued in a plateglass pane
    reddened in the reflection

of the red Triomphe
parked at the edge of the sea

the sea glittering in the sun
the swirls of nebula

in the espresso cup
raindrops, neon spectra

on a vinyl raincoat

3.   To love, to move perpetually
as the body changes

a dozen times a day
the temperature of the skin

the feeling of rise & fall
deadweight & buoyancy

the eye sunk inward
the eye bleeding with speech

('for that moment at least
I wás you—')

To be stopped, to shoot the same scene
over & over

4.   At the end of *Alphaville*
she says *I love you*

and the film begins
that you've said you'd never make

because it's impossible
'things as difficult to show

as horror & war & sickness are'

meaning: love,
to speak in the mouth

to touch the breast
for a woman

to know the sex of a man
That film begins here

yet you don't show it
we leave the theatre

suffering from that

5.   Interior monologue of the poet:
     the notes for the poem are the only poem

     the mind collecting, devouring
     all these destructibles

     the unmade studio couch the air
     shifting the abalone shells

     the mind of the poet is the only poem
     the poet is at the movies

     dreaming the film-maker's dream but differently
     free in the dark as if asleep

     free in the dusty beam of the projector
     the mind of the poet is changing

     the moment of change is the only poem

1970

A Valediction Forbidding Mourning

My swirling wants. Your frozen lips.
The grammar turned and attacked me.
Themes, written under duress.
Emptiness of the notations.

They gave me a drug that slowed the healing of wounds.

I want you to see this before I leave:
the experience of repetition as death
the failure of criticism to locate the pain
the poster in the bus that said:
my bleeding is under control.

A red plant in a cemetery of plastic wreaths.

A last attempt: the language is a dialect called metaphor.
These images go unglossed: hair, glacier, flashlight.
When I think of a landscape I am thinking of a time.
When I talk of taking a trip I mean forever.
I could say: those mountains have a meaning
but further than that I could not say.

To do something very common, in my own way.

1970

Shooting Script

PART I

11/69–2/70

1.

We were bound on the wheel of an endless conversation.

Inside this shell, a tide waiting for someone to enter.

A monologue waiting for you to interrupt it.

A man wading into the surf. The dialogue of the rock with the breaker.

The wave changed instantly by the rock; the rock changed by the wave returning over and over.

The dialogue that lasts all night or a whole lifetime.

A conversation of sounds melting constantly into rhythms.

A shell waiting for you to listen.

A tide that ebbs and flows against a deserted continent.

A cycle whose rhythm begins to change the meanings of words.

A wheel of blinding waves of light, the spokes pulsing out from where we hang together in the turning of an endless conversation.

The meaning that searches for its word like a hermit crab.

A monologue that waits for one listener.

An ear filled with one sound only.

A shell penetrated by meaning.

2.

(*Adapted from
Mirza Ghalib*)

Even when I thought I prayed, I was talking to myself; when I
found the door shut, I simply walked away.

We all accept Your claim to be unique; the stone lips, the
carved limbs, were never your true portrait.

Grief held back from the lips wears at the heart; the drop that
refused to join the river dried up in the dust.

Now tell me your story till the blood drips from your lashes. Any
other version belongs to your folklore, or ours.

To see the Tigris in a water-drop . . . Either you were playing
games with me, or you never cared to learn the structure of my
language.

3.

The old blanket. The crumbs of rubbed wool turning up.

Where we lay and breakfasted. The stains of tea. The squares of winter light projected on the wool.

You, sleeping with closed windows. I, sleeping in the silver nitrate burn of zero air.

Where it can snow, I'm at home; the crystals accumulating spell out my story.

The cold encrustation thickening on the ledge.

The arrow-headed facts, accumulating, till a whole city is taken over.

Midwinter and the loss of love, going comes before gone, over and over the point is missed and still the blind will turns for its target.

4.

In my imagination I was the pivot of a fresh beginning.

In rafts they came over the sea; on the island they put up those stones by methods we can only guess at.

If the vegetation grows as thick as this, how can we see what they were seeing?

It is all being made clear, with bulldozers, at Angkor Wat.

The verdure was a false mystery; the baring of the stones is no solution for us now.

Defoliation progresses; concrete is poured, sheets of glass hauled overland in huge trucks and at great cost.

Here we never travailed, never took off our shoes to walk the final mile.

Come and look into this cellar-hole; this is the foundling of the woods.

Humans lived here once; it became sacred only when they went away.

5.

Of simple choice they are the villagers; their clothes come with them like red clay roads they have been walking.

The sole of the foot is a map, the palm of the hand a letter, learned by heart and worn close to the body.

They seemed strange to me, till I began to recall their dialect.

Poking the spade into the dry loam, listening for the tick of broken pottery, hoarding the brown and black bits in a dented can.

Evenings, at the table, turning the findings out, pushing them around with a finger, beginning to dream of fitting them together.

Hiding all this work from them, although they might have helped me.

Going up at night, hiding the tin can in a closet, where the linoleum lies in shatters on a back shelf.

Sleeping to dream of the unformed, the veil of water pouring over the wet clay, the rhythms of choice, the lost methods.

6.

You are beside me like a wall; I touch you with my fingers and keep moving through the bad light.

At this time of year when faces turn aside, it is amazing that your eyes are to be met.

A bad light is one like this, that flickers and diffuses itself along the edge of a frontier.

No, I don't invest you with anything; I am counting on your weakness as much as on your strength.

This light eats away at the clarities I had fixed on; it moves up like a rodent at the edge of the raked paths.

Your clarities may not reach me; but your attention will.

It is to know that I too have no mythic powers; it is to see the liability of all my treasures.

You will have to see all this for a long time alone.

You are beside me like a wall; I touch you with my fingers and keep trying to move through the bad light.

7.

Picking the wax to crumbs in the iron lip of the candelabrum.

Fingering down the thread of the maze where the green strand cuts across the violet strand.

Picking apart the strands of pain; a warp of wool dipped in burning wax.

When the flame shrinks to a blue bead, there is danger; the change of light in a flickering situation.

Stretched on the loom the light expands; the smell of a smell of burning.

When the change leaves you dark, when the wax cools in the socket, when I thought I prayed, when I was talking to myself under the cover of my darkness.

Someone who never said, "What do you feel?" someone who sat across from me, taking the crumbs of wax as I picked them apart and handed them over.

PART II

3–7/70

8.

(For Hugh Seidman.

A woman waking behind grimed blinds slatted across a courtyard she never looks into.

Thinking of the force of a waterfall, the slash of cold air from the thickest water of the falls, slicing the green and ochre afternoon in which he turns his head and walks away.

Thinking of that place as an existence.

A woman reaching for the glass of water left all night on the bureau, the half-done poem, the immediate relief.

Entering the poem as a method of leaving the room.

Entering the paper airplane of the poem, which somewhere before its destination starts curling into ash and comes apart.

The woman is too heavy for the poem, she is a swolleness, a foot, an arm, gone asleep, grown absurd and out of bounds.

Rooted to memory like a wedge in a block of wood; she takes the pressure of her thought but cannot resist it.

You call this a poetry of false problems, the shotgun wedding of the mind, the subversion of choice by language.

Instead of the alternative: to pull the sooty strings to set the window bare to purge the room with light to feel the sun breaking in on the courtyard and the steamheat smothering in the shut-off pipes.

To feel existence as this time, this place, the pathos and force of the lumps of snow gritted and melting in the unloved corners of the courtyard.

9.

(Newsreel)

This would not be the war we fought in. See, the foliage is
heavier, there were no hills of that size there.

But I find it impossible not to look for actual persons known
to me and not seen since; impossible not to look for myself.

The scenery angers me, I know there is something wrong, the sun
is too high, the grass too trampled, the peasants' faces too broad,
and the main square of the capital had no arcades like those.

Yet the dead look right, and the roofs of the huts, and the crashed
fuselage burning among the ferns.

But this is not the war I came to see, buying my ticket, stumbling
through the darkness, finding my place among the sleepers and
masturbators in the dark.

I thought of seeing the General who cursed us, whose name they
gave to an expressway; I wanted to see the faces of the dead when
they were living.

Once I know they filmed us, back at the camp behind the lines,
taking showers under the trees and showing pictures of our girls.

Somewhere there is a film of the war we fought in, and it must
contain the flares, the souvenirs, the shadows of the netted brush,
the standing in line of the innocent, the hills that were not of
this size.

Somewhere my body goes taut under the deluge, somewhere I am
naked behind the lines, washing my body in the water of that war.

Someone has that war stored up in metal canisters, a memory he
cannot use, somewhere my innocence is proven with my guilt, but
this would not be the war I fought in.

10.

(For Valerie Glauber.

They come to you with their descriptions of your soul.

They come and drop their mementoes at the foot of your bed; their feathers, ferns, fans, grasses from the western mountains.

They wait for you to unfold for them like a paper flower, a secret springing open in a glass of water.

They believe your future has a history and that it is themselves.

They have family trees to plant for you, photographs of dead children, old bracelets and rings they want to fasten onto you.

And, in spite of this, you live alone.

Your secret hangs in the open like Poe's purloined letter; their longing and their methods will never let them find it.

Your secret cries out in the dark and hushes; when they start out of sleep they think you are innocent.

You hang among them like the icon in a Russian play; living your own intenser life behind the lamp they light in front of you.

You are spilt here like mercury on a marble counter, liquefying into many globes, each silvered like a planet caught in a lens.

You are a mirror lost in a brook, an eye reflecting a torrent of reflections.

You are a letter written, folded, burnt to ash, and mailed in an envelope to another continent.

11.

The mare's skeleton in the clearing: another sign of life.

When you pull the embedded bones up from the soil, the flies collect again.

The pelvis, the open archway, staring at me like an eye.

In the desert these bones would be burnt white; a green bloom grows on them in the woods.

Did she break her leg or die of poison?

What was it like when the scavengers came?

So many questions unanswered, yet the statement is here and clear.

With what joy you handled the skull, set back the teeth spilt in the grass, hinged back the jaw on the jaw.

With what joy we left the woods, swinging our sticks, miming the speech of noble savages, of the fathers of our country, bursting into the full sun of the uncut field.

12.

I was looking for a way out of a lifetime's consolations.

We walked in the wholesale district: closed warehouses, windows, steeped in sun.

I said: those cloths are very old.   You said: they have lain in that window a long time.

When the skeletons of the projects shut off the sunset, when the sense of the Hudson leaves us, when only by loss of light in the east do I know that I am living in the west.

When I give up being paraphrased, when I let go, when the beautiful solutions in their crystal flasks have dried up in the sun, when the lightbulb bursts on lighting, when the dead bulb rattles like a seed-pod.

Those cloths are very old, they are mummies' cloths, they have lain in graves, they were not intended to be sold, the tragedy of this mistake will soon be clear.

Vacillant needles of Manhattan, describing hour & weather; buying these descriptions at the cost of missing every other point.

13.

We are driven to odd attempts; once it would not have occurred to me to put out in a boat, not on a night like this.

Still, it was an instrument, and I had pledged myself to try any instrument that came my way. Never to refuse one from conviction of incompetence.

A long time I was simply learning to handle the skiff; I had no special training and my own training was against me.

I had always heard that darkness and water were a threat.

In spite of this, darkness and water helped me to arrive here.

I watched the lights on the shore I had left for a long time; each one, it seemed to me, was a light I might have lit, in the old days.

14.

Whatever it was: the grains of the glacier caked in the boot-cleats; ashes spilled on white formica.

The death-col viewed through power-glasses; the cube of ice melting on stainless steel.

Whatever it was, the image that stopped you, the one on which you came to grief, projecting it over & over on empty walls.

Now to give up the temptations of the projector; to see instead the web of cracks filtering across the plaster.

To read there the map of the future, the roads radiating from the initial split, the filaments thrown out from that impasse.

To reread the instructions on your palm; to find there how the lifeline, broken, keeps its direction.

To read the etched rays of the bullet-hole left years ago in the glass; to know in every distortion of the light what fracture is.

To put the prism in your pocket, the thin glass lens, the map of the inner city, the little book with gridded pages.

To pull yourself up by your own roots; to eat the last meal in your old neighborhood.